# Horses

Tammy Gagne

PURPLE TOAD
PUBLISHING

P.O. Box 631
Kennett Square, Pennsylvania 19348
www.purpletoadpublishing.com

Printing     1          2          3          4          5          6          7          8          9

A TOMMY TIGER book

## WHAT ARE THEY SAYING?

Birds
Cats
Dogs
Guinea Pigs
Horses

**Publisher's Congress-in-Publication Data**
Gagne, Tammy
  Horses / Tammy Gagne
      p. cm. – (A Tommy tiger book. What are they saying)
Includes bibliographic references and index.
ISBN: 978-1-62469-007-5 (library bound)
1. Horses – Juvenile literature.     I. Title.
  SF302.G3464 2013
  636.1 – dc23
                                                                                2013930994

eBook ISBN: 978-1-62469-018-1

**ABOUT THE AUTHOR:** Tammy Gagne is a freelance writer who has authored numerous books for both adults and children. In her spare time, she enjoys visiting schools to speak to children about the writing process. She resides in northern New England with her husband, son, and a menagerie of animals.

**PUBLISHER'S NOTE:** The data in this book has been researched in depth, and to the best of our knowledge is factual. Although every measure has been taken to give an accurate account, Purple Toad Publishing makes no warranty of the accuracy of the information and is not liable for damages caused by inaccuracies.

Printed by Lake Book Manufacturing, Chicago, IL

# Horses

I can't curl up on your lap or play fetch, but I CAN carry you on my back and gallop over fields.
I love to run, feeling the wind whistle through my mane.
I LOVE being a horse!

I am a very social animal who enjoys spending time with people and other horses.
I communicate using sounds and movement.

Pet Fact:

social (SOH-shuhl)—
Friendly.

nicker (NIK-er)—A soft sound a horse makes through its nostrils. Horses are herbivores, which means they only eat plants.

6

Most horses begin each day with a noise called a nicker. When we make this sound through our nostrils, we are saying, "Hello! I'm so happy to see you."

I may also make this sound when you enter the barn—and not just because you are bringing me breakfast. I use this greeting for people and animals I like the most.

When you look at me, you may notice that my ears are almost always moving.
I can hear many sounds that people cannot.
My ears tell me when a person or animal is approaching.
I can move them in different directions at the same time.

Since I have one eye on each side of my head, sometimes it can be difficult to tell where I am looking.

One way to tell is by watching my ears. If they are both pointed forward, I am most likely looking straight ahead.

If one ear is pointed to the side, I am probably looking in that direction.

**Pet Fact:**

Horses have the largest eyes of any land mammal. With their eyes on the sides of their heads, they can see almost all the way around, front to back, at once.

I can also use my ears to tell you what I am feeling.
When I listen to something behind me, I hold my ears back. If I am holding them back tightly, watch out. I might be getting ready to bite or kick. I usually hold my ears forward when I am relaxed. When I am paying close attention to something, I will prick them even farther forward.
I also do this when I'm frightened.

when I was younger, I did something called snapping when I was scared.
I would open and close my mouth over and over.
I did this when a bigger horse came near me.
Snapping was my way of saying, "I'm just a foal. Please don't hurt me."

Pet Fact:

Horses can gallop at 30 miles per hour!

snap—A nervous movement consisting of opening and closing the mouth repeatedly.

**Pet Fact:**

neigh (NEY)—The loudest noise a horse makes; also called a whinny.

Now when I am frightened, I may snort.
If I want to warn a fellow horse that there is danger nearby, I will neigh.
But I also neigh when playing with my friends or to let my caregiver know that it's past my dinnertime.
Some people also call this sound a whinny.
If I make a high-pitched squeal, it usually means that I am angry.
If I am really upset, I will kick my hind legs.

**Pet Fact:**

body language (BOD-ee LANG-gwij)—
A way of showing thoughts and
feelings through movements.

Horses use body language more often than sounds to communicate with other horses and with people.

I hold my head high when I am feeling alert. When I'm calm, I usually lower my head a bit.

I can use my tail to show several different feelings.
If I carry it high, I am feeling confident.
If I hold it tightly against my rear end, I am afraid.
If I am swishing it like a cat, I am irritated.
I am not wagging my tail.

Never walk near the rear of a horse or you might scare him and he'll kick in fright. A tail swish might mean to back away.

Horses use their tails to swat nagging flies and to send signals to other horses about how they feel.

Horses' hooves don't get cold in snow as do the feet of people.

When I am REALLY happy, I love to roll.
It may look pretty silly to see me on
my back with my legs kicking in
the air,
but it scratches that itch!

I love to be groomed! As my owner brushes gently over my tired muscles, I let him know how relaxed and good I feel by licking and chewing.
If I want a massage, I may lean into the curry comb. I might even yawn from pleasure and relaxation.

**Pet Fact:**

Use a curry comb to loosen dirt and massage the horse, but use a dandy brush to sweep the dirt off. A soft body brush works well on delicate areas. It also makes the horse shine.

Curry comb

Dandy brush

When I have the space and I feel safe, I like to sleep lying flat on my side.

Most horses won't lie this way for more than about half an hour.

If you are lucky enough to catch me in this position, you might see twitching or my legs moving.

These movements are signs that I am dreaming.

Pet Fact:

Horses can dream they are running and maybe even swimming!

Horses spend a lot less time sleeping than people do. Most horses sleep about three hours each night, but we don't sleep for three hours all at once. Instead, we nod off for several minutes at a time. Unlike a person, we can also sleep while standing on our feet.

We can see very well at night so we sometimes like to give folks a ride before bedtime.

Pet Fact:

Horses can see just as well in darkness as a person with normal sight can in full sunlight.

29

Even if you don't have a horse of your own, you can understand what we are saying through our sounds and movements. This can help us become lifelong friends.

**Books**

Eschbach, Andrea and Marcus. *How to Speak Horse: A Horse-Crazy Kid's Guide to Reading Body Language and "Talking Back."* North Pomfret, Vermont: Trafalgar Square Books, 2012.

Hill, Cherry. *Cherry Hill's Horse Care for Kids.* Adams, Massachusetts: Storey Publishing, 2002.

Vogel, Colin. *Complete Horse Care Manual.* New York, New York: DK Publishing, 2011.

**Works Consulted**

Hempfling, Klaus Ferdinand. *It's Not I Who Seeks the Horse, the Horse Seeks Me: My Path to an Understanding of Equine Body Language.* Richmond, United Kingdom: Cadmos Books, 2010.

Hill, Cherry. *How To Think Like A Horse.* Adams, Massachusetts: Storey Publishing, 2006.

McBane, Susan. *Horse and Pony Body Language Phrasebook.* San Diego, California: Thunder Bay Press, 2008.

McFarland, Cynthia. "Equine Body Language." HorseChannel.com. http://www.horsechannel.com/horse-keeping/horse-body-language.aspx

Scott, Laurel. "Equine Expressions: Understanding Your Horse's Body Language." Practical Horseman, April 1, 2009.

**On the Internet**

Breeds of Livestock (horses) http://www.ansi.okstate.edu/breeds/horses/

Everything Horse and Pony for Kids http://www.squidoo.com/HorsePony4Kids

Pony Club http://www.ponyclub.org/

## INDEX

afraid  12, 14, 17, 20, 21
alert  19
angry  12, 17
body language  18, 19, 30
calm  19, 24
confident  20
dreaming  26, 27
ears  8, 11, 12
eyes  11, 29
happy  7, 23
hooves  22
hungry  17
kicking  12, 17, 21, 23

neighing  16, 17
nickering  6, 7
playing  17
rolling  23
sleeping  26, 29
snapping  14
snorting  17
social  5
squealing  17
tail  20, 21
whinnying  16, 17
yawning  24